The Val... ...f M...

COUNTING
COIN$
AND BILL$

PORTIA SUMMERS

Enslow Publishing
101 W. 23rd Street
Suite 240
New York, NY 10011
USA

enslow.com

WORDS TO KNOW

amount—How much of something there is.
bill—Paper money.
count—To add up or put together.
currency—The kind of money a country uses.
decimal—A period that represents a separation between a full number and a fraction of it.
dollar—The American currency.
value—The worth of something.

CONTENTS

A QUICK LOOK AT MONEY

penny	nickel	dime	quarter	half-dollar	one-dollar coin
1¢	5¢	10¢	25¢	50¢	$1

one-dollar bill
$1

five-dollar bill
$5

ten-dollar bill
$10

twenty-dollar bill
$20

COUNTING MATCHING COINS

Five pennies = 5¢.

1¢   2¢   3¢   4¢   5¢

One nickel = 5¢. You count nickels by fives.

5¢   10¢   15¢   20¢

Four nickels = 20¢.

One dime = 10¢. You count dimes by tens.

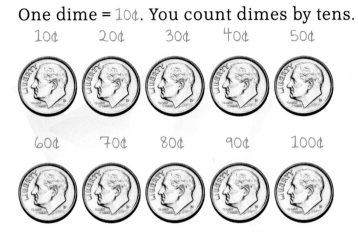

10¢   20¢   30¢   40¢   50¢

60¢   70¢   80¢   90¢   100¢

Ten dimes = 100¢.

You count quarters by twenty-fives.
Four quarters make 100¢.

25¢   50¢   75¢   100¢

100¢ = $1.00

PENNIES, NICKELS, AND DIMES

One way to figure out how much different coins are worth is to count the most valuable coins first. Count nickels before pennies.

What is the value of 2 nickels and 4 pennies? Count the nickels first.

5¢ + 5¢ = 10¢

Now, count one for each penny.

11¢   12¢   13¢   14¢ = 14¢

The total value of the coins is 14¢.

What is the value of 4 nickels and 3 pennies?

5¢   10¢   15¢   20¢   21¢   22¢   23¢

Legend says that Martha Washington, the wife of the first president, George Washington, gave up the silverware from her table in order for it to be melted down for the first US currency. She is also the only woman to have appeared on US bills. In the 1800s, she was on the one-dollar bill.

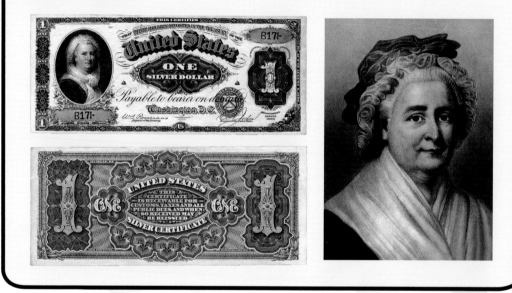

One dime = 10¢.

What is the value of 2 dimes and 3 nickels?
First, count the dimes.

10¢   10¢   =   20¢

Then, count the nickels by five.

25¢   30¢   35¢

The coins equal 35¢.

What is the value of 2 dimes, 2 nickels, and 4 pennies?
Count the dimes first.

10¢   +   10¢   = 20¢

Then count the nickels by five.

25¢   30¢

Then, count the pennies.

31¢   32¢   33¢   34¢   =34¢

COUNTING QUARTERS

One quarter = 25¢.
What is the value of 2 quarters and 3 dimes?

Count the quarters first.

25¢   +   25¢   = 50¢

Then, count ten for each dime.

60¢　　70¢　　80¢

You have a total of 80¢.

Moments in Minting

When coins get worn out, they are melted down and made into new coins.

What is the value of 2 quarters, 3 dimes, 3 nickels, and 4 pennies?

Count the quarters first.

25¢   50¢

Count the dimes by tens.

60¢   70¢   80¢

Count the nickels by fives.

85¢   90¢   95¢

Count one more for each penny.

96¢   97¢   98¢   99¢

The total value is 99¢.

HOW TO MAKE AN AMOUNT

You can use coins to make a certain amount, too.
What coins can you use to make 86¢?
Three quarters make 75¢.
Add one dime to make 85¢.
Add one penny and you have 86¢.

25¢　　　50¢　　　75¢

85¢　　　86¢

What other coins could you use to make 86¢?
Eight dimes makes 80¢.

One nickel equals 5¢. So 80¢ + 5¢ = 85¢

One penny equals 1¢. So 85¢ + 1¢ = 86¢

Eight dimes, a nickel, and a penny equals 86¢.

To make an amount using the least number of coins, you'll have to use the most valuable coins first.

Make 42¢ using the least number of coins you can.

Can you use quarters? One quarter is 25¢.

Two are 50¢, which is more than you're trying to make. So only use one.

Can you use dimes? You already have 25¢ from the quarter. Add one dime.

25¢ + 10¢ = 35¢

But add one more dime, and you're up to 45¢. You're only trying to reach 42¢.

Can you use any nickels? You already have 35¢. Add one nickel.

35¢ + 5¢ = 40¢

But adding another nickel makes it 45¢, which is too much. Only use one nickel.

Can you use any pennies? You already have 40¢.

40¢ + 1¢ + 1¢ = 42¢

The least number of coins to equal 42¢ is one quarter, one dime, one nickel, and two pennies.

COUNTING MORE THAN A DOLLAR

Money values are written using a dollar sign ($) and a decimal point (.).

$1.34

Numbers on the left side of the decimal point stand for dollars. Numbers on the right stand for cents.

When you say a money amount out loud, you say the dollars first. Say "and" at the decimal point, followed by the cents. So $1.34 would be read aloud "One dollar and thirty-four cents."

What is the value of five quarters and one penny? Count the values out loud.

25¢ "twenty-five cents"
50¢ "fifty cents"
75¢ "seventy-five cents"
$1.00 "one dollar"
$1.25 "one dollar and twenty-five cents"
$1.26 "one dollar and twenty-six cents"

The total value is $1.26.

COUNTING BILLS

You count the value of bills the same way you would coins. Count the most valuable ones first.

What is the value of the bills shown?

Count the twenty-dollar bills first. There are two. The value so far is $40.00.

Count the ten-dollar bills. There are four. Start from forty and count ten for each ten-dollar bill you see.
40   50   60   70   80.
The total so far is $80.00.

Count the five-dollar bills. There are two.

Moments in Minting

The first paper money was used in China more than 1,400 years ago.

Count five for every five-dollar bill.

80   85   90

The total so far is $90.

Count the one-dollar bills. There are three. For every $1.00 you see, count one.

90   91   92   93

The total of all the bills is $93.00.

COUNTING BILLS AND COINS

Bills and coins are often counted together by counting the bills first, then the coins. Start with the most valuable bills first.

What is the value of the money here?

There are two ten-dollar bills. Count ten for each.
10   20
The total so far is $20.00.

There are three five-dollar bills. Count five for each.
20   25   30   35
So far the total is $35.00.

How many one-dollar bills do you see? Count one for each.
35   36   37   38   39
The total value of the bills is $39.00.

Now, count the coins. There are two quarters. Count twenty-five for each.
25   50

There is one dime. Count ten for it.
50   60

There are no nickels. But there are three pennies. Count one for each.
60   61   62   63

The total value of the coins is 63¢.

Now combine the value of the bills and the value of the coins.

The total value is $39.63. Read it as "thirty-nine dollars and sixty-three cents."

Find the value of this amount of money.

There is one twenty-dollar bill. So far, the value is $20.00. There are no ten-dollar bills, but there is a five-dollar bill. Count five.

20   25

There is one one-dollar bill. Count one more.

25   26

There are no quarters. But there are three dimes.

10   20   30

There are two nickels. Count five for each.

30   35   40

There is one penny. Count one.

40   41

Combine the value of the bills with the value of the coins. The total value is $26.41. Read it as "twenty-six dollars and forty-one cents."

Now practice counting bills and coins. See how much money is in your pocket or your piggy bank!

LEARN MORE

BOOKS

Cleary, Brian P. *A Dollar, a Penny, How Much and How Many?* Minneapolis, MN: Lerner Publications, 2015.

Domnauer, Teresa. *Money Mania Stick Kids Workbook.* Cypress, CA: Creative Teaching Press, 2012.

Marsico, Katie. *Money Math.* Minneapolis, MN: Lerner Classroom, 2015.

WEBSITES

H.I.P. Pocket Change

www.usmint.gov/kids

Read about the history of the United States Mint, play games, and watch cartoons.

ABCYa.com

www.abcya.com/learning_coins.htm

Learn about US coins and dollar bills and play a sorting game.

INDEX

Published in 2017 by Enslow Publishing, LLC.
101 W. 23rd Street, Suite 240, New York, NY 10011

Library of Congress Cataloging-in-Publication Data
Name: Summers, Portia, author.
Title: Counting coins and bills / Portia Summers.
Description: New York, NY : Enslow Publishing, 2017. | 2017. | Series: The value of money | Audience: Ages 6+ | Audience: K to grade 3. | Includes bibliographical references and index.
Identifiers: LCCN 2015046101| ISBN 9780766077041 (library bound) | ISBN 9780766077003 (pbk.) | ISBN 9780766077034 (6-pack).
Subjects: LCSH: Money--Juvenile literature. | Counting--Juvenile literature.
Classification: LCC HG221.5 .S855 2017 | DDC 332.4--dc23
LC record available at http://lccn.loc.gov/2015046101

Printed in Malaysia

To Our Readers: We have done our best to make sure all website adressess in this book were active and appropriate when we went to press. However, the author and the publisher have no control over and assume no liability for the material available on those websites or on any websites they may link to. Any comments or suggestions can be sent by e-mail to customerservice@enslow.com.

Portions of this book originally appeared in the book *I Can Count Money* by Rebecca Wingard-Nelson.

Photo Credits: Cover (green dollar sign background, used throughout the book) Rachael Arnott/Shutterstock.com, Fedorov Oleksiy/Shutterstock.com; (white dollar sign background, used throughout the book) Golden Shrimp/Shutterstock.com; VIGE.COM/Shutterstock.com (piggy bank with dollar sign, used throughout book); Golden Shrimp/Shutterstock.com (green cross pattern border, used throughout book); p. 2 yurchello108/Shutterstock.com; p. 3 RomanR/Shutterstock.com; p. 4 penny (used throughout the book), mattesimages/Shutterstock.com; nickel (used throughout the book), United States Mint image; dime and quarter (used throughout the book), B Brown/Shutterstock.com; half-dollar, Daniel D Malone/Shutterstock.com; one-dollar coin, JordiDelgado/iStockphoto.com; one-dollar, five-dollar and twenty-dollar bills (used throuout the book) Anton_Ivanov/Shutterstock.com; ten-dollar bill, Pavel Kirichenko/Shutterstock.com; p. 5, 10, 16 JGI/Jamie Grill/Blend Images/Getty Images; p. 8 (left) National Numismatic Collection at the Smithsonian Institution/File:US-$1-SC-1886-Fr.215.jpg/Wikimedia Commons; (right) John Chester Buttre (1821–1893), engraver, after Gilbert Stuart/Library of Congress/File:Martha Washington.png/Wikimedia Commons; p. 9 Frank van Delf/Cultura/Getty Images; p. 11 Auscape/UIG/Getty Images; p. 13 McIninch/iStockphoto.com; p. 18 Anne-Marie Weber/Taxi//Getty Images.